LIVING IN RHYME

LIVING IN RHYME IS COLLECTION OF POEMS THAT DEFINES THE SWEETEST AND BITTER TRUTHS OF LIFE.

ASIM ZULFIQAR

Table of Contents

Poem 1. ANIMALS

Poem 2. MY LOVELY CHILDHOOD

Poem 3. MIDNIGHT

Poem 4. DECEMBER

Poem 5. DID YOU REMEMBER ?

Poem 6. PROMISE

Poem 7. WHY WE ARE BORN ?

Poem 8. I WISH.

Poem 9. THE LONELY WOMAN

Poem 10. THE TRUTH BEHIND MY SMILING FACE

About The Poet

POEM 1. ANIMALS

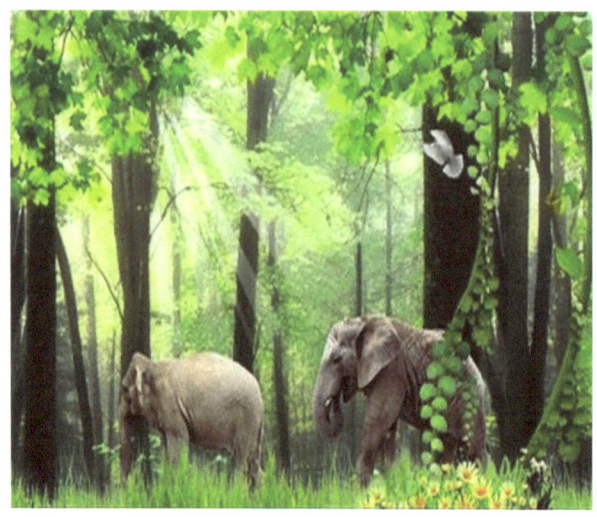

God had made us superior,
but none of his creature is inferior,

we may rule the universe,
or might reach the Jupiter.

but we are nothing without them,
we are prospering because of them.

is there anyone more loyal than the dog?
can u find more loyalty among any soul?

donkey is active and do hard work,
no attitude and better than our clerks.

we can be sports car expert,
but can u beat camel in a desert?

the cow gives u the milk,
which makes your hairs silk?

the little bee gives u the honey,
which u can't produce with the money?

zebra, monkey and birds,
teach u the team works.

all the good things which we call manners,
we have got ideas from their reactions.

yes,

God had made us superior,
but none of his creature is inferior,

we may rule the universe,
or might reach the Jupiter.

but we are nothing without them,

we are prospering because of them.

POEM 2. MY LOVELY CHILDHOOD

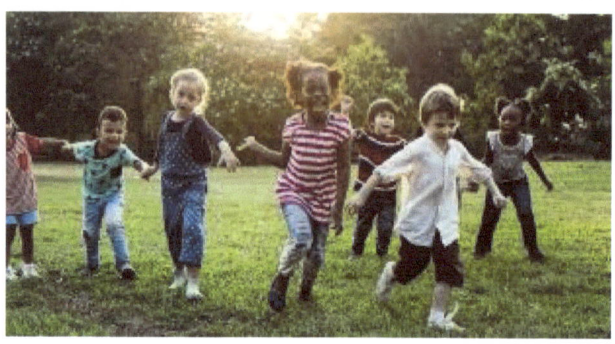

I wanna go back to the time,
When everything was fine,
Going bed early at nine.
There was no trouble of science,
Playing games with my toys.

Jerry was my friend, teddy my bestie.
Blue was my car, which beat every nasty.
Dirty my Clothes, lights on my shoes.
Every one shouts oh my moon...

Life was easy, and the days were cool,
Fighting on little things and writing cards soon,
Head on mom's lap, my every wish comes TRUE.
I wanna go back to the time,
when everything was mine.

Favorite song was twinkle twinkle and love bean,
Crying loud to fulfill our dream,
Sorry thanks was nothing, smile was the key,
love was when my mom kisses me and dad holds my hand,
It was fun no tension at the end.

I wanna go back to the time,
When everything was fine.

POEM 3. MIDNIGHT

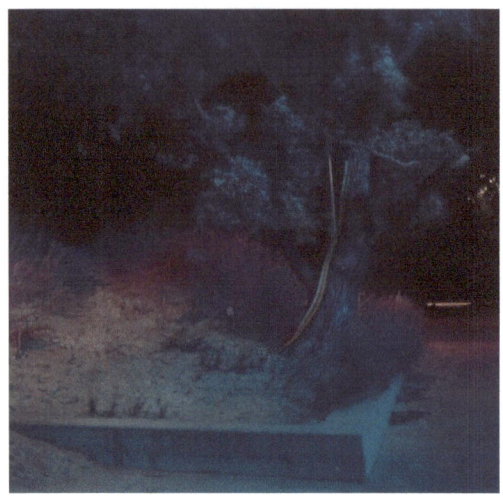

I wake up in the middle of night,
you would have been gone , that was my fright,
I was guilt , why I had lied ,
I was thinking why I had not tried ?

You had told me you will never go .
The sun of our love will always glow,
thinking that makes my mind blow ,
I love you , tell me how I show ?

fighting with memories in the mid of night ,
I can't see any hope far and wide ,
I wish you have not left so you can guide,
baby , you forgot ? you were my pride .

I wake up in the middle of night,

you would have been gone , that was my fright,
I wish I could cry , but my tears are dried,
miss you a lot , see I have cried.

you told me that you are always by my side,
I'll put ring in your finger , and you'll be my bride,
thinking that broke me inside,
I love you , you can't denied ,

memorizing memories in the mid of night ,
I wish you were here in my sight,
I can't breathe , this is making me quite,
where you can escape , remember I am your type,

I wake up in the middle of night,
you would have been gone , that was my fright,
I was guilt , why I had lied ,
I was thinking why I had not tried ?

POEM 4. DECEMBER

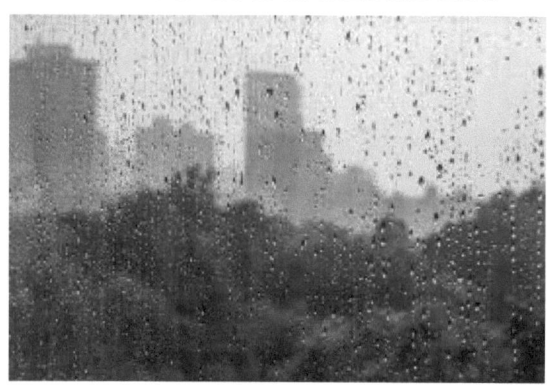

sitting at the edge of chair, Starring at the mirror,
her hands on my shoulder, and she disappears,
Weather getting cold , drinking beer,
days are getting darker and forever,

you called me at 3 a.m. , and it was December,
decided to move on, since then I remembered ,
all I could do was to surrender,
you forgot we were going to live together,

you have gone like sunshine,
leaving me alone ,propping on whine,
you told me that you were mine,
and you left , leaving no sign.

All I have now is a month of December,
Few memories which I had remembered,

you loves me , you were pretender,
since then I have not found heart mender.

POEM 5. DID YOU REMEMBER?

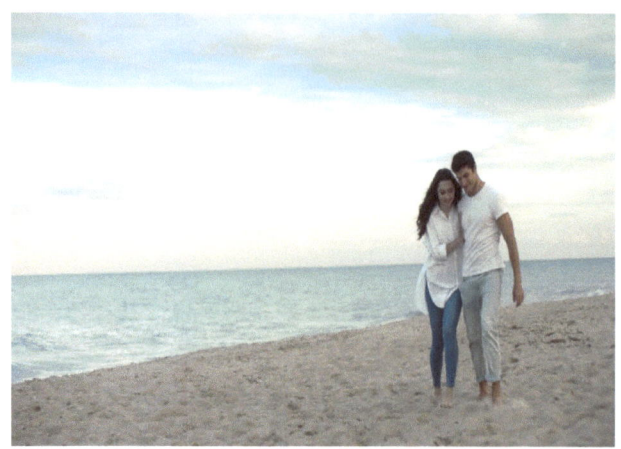

Everything happens for a reason,
but now it's a grief season,
I don't know what's good in this,
from her sadness to her bliss,

Did you remember I proposed you?
i remember you were dressed in blue,

Did you remember your birthday?
we had made our house with clay,

Did you remember the new year?
You told me that you will be my dear,

Everything happens for a reason,
but now it's a grief season,
i don't know what's good in this,
from her sadness to her bliss,

Did you remember that party on beach?
you, me and shadow of each,

Did you remember that candle light dinner?
and you asked me how you were looking in front of mirror,

did you remember that strawberry ice-cream?
hand in hand, and all of our dreams,

Everything happens for a reason,
but now it's a grief season,
i don't know what's good in this,
from her sadness to her bliss,

everything messed, you were missed,
but i can't forget our life's that list.

POEM 6. PROMISE

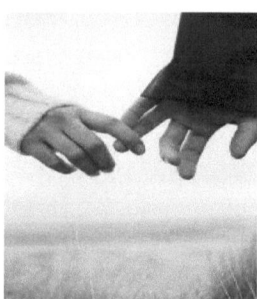

let me do a promise with you,
but before that baby please dress in blue.

the weather is not romantic,
so let me pray to god that please make it antic ,

see the clouds have appeared and it's going to be raining ,
baby please fast , it's the moment I was planning .

give me your hand , drown in my eyes ,
your shiny hair band , I will lift your thigh ,

now look , I can't live without you ,
in my book you have the best view ,

your eyes are like a blue lake ,
I promise I will not be fake .

your nose is like a red ball ,
I promise I will never let you fall .

your hairs are shinny and silky ,
I promise I will never make you guilty .

your lips are…..look it's raining ,
I will come nearer and my heart shaking .

you will be happy in my tiny world ,
because you are the one I call my dove

POEM 7. WHY WE ARE BORN?

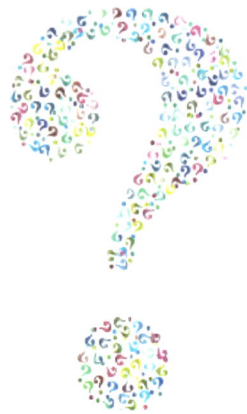

have you ever wonder why you were born ?
why the earth, planets, skies, life was formed ?

is this the mystery or the secret of lord ?
we might be here to let the universe explored .
imagine the world without humans ,
from that one thing can be proven ,
the world will not be world but heaven ,

we are the inventor of tension ,
have forgotten the god's lesson,
and still looking for good future and present,
our life had become sins session ,
and still looking for the heaven ,

have you ever wonder why you were born ?
why the earth, planets, skies, life was formed ?

we are born to let the Gods principle restored,
don't forget one day we will have to report,
and we will be standing in the God's court,
but here in the world we are lost ,
because we had forgotten why we are born.

POEM 8. I WISH

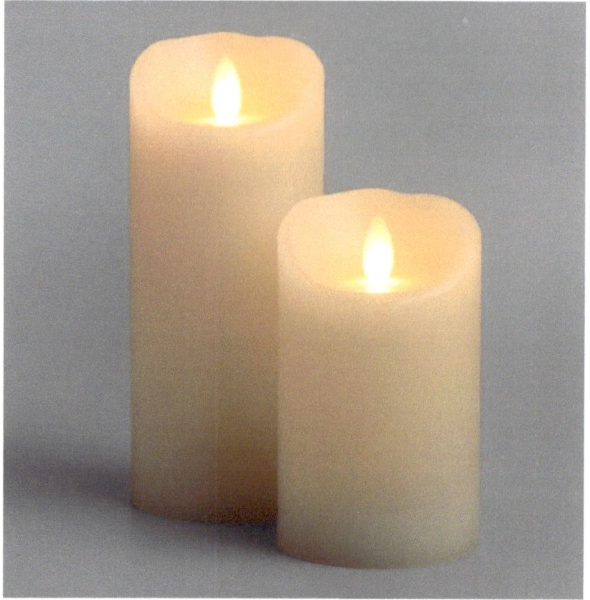

I wish she could hear my voice,
as it was not my last choice,

I wish she could watch my face,
I was alive that time I guess,

I wish she could kiss my chicks,
and could wash all the conflicts,

I wish she could hold my hand,
and my life would be her demand,

I wish I could live more,
and I could make her happy for sure,

I wish, I wish ....
and here drown my fish

POEM 9. A LONELY WOMAN

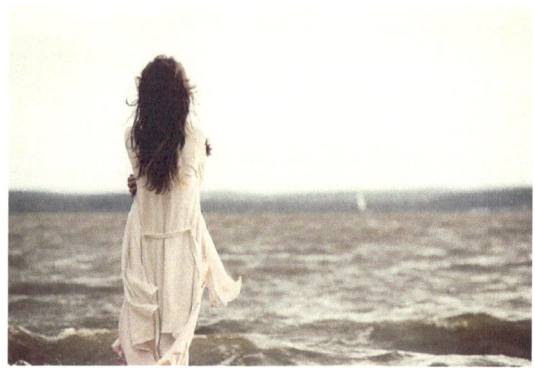

I saw a woman sitting along the highway ,
she was waiting for someone or might be astray,
tired or might be she was betrayed .
was trying to smile or might be pushing sorrows away ,

I was seeing her from the other side ,
she must be in trouble ,I compiled.
I crossed the road to let her guide.
I greet her ,but she didn't replied.

she was in the deep thought ,
about all the lessons life had taught ,
and all the things she had got ,
I was confused at that spot ,

suddenly the noise of truck makes her out of situation,
she saw me as noise breaks her concentration ,

I asked her can I know the reason of your depression ?
or may I guide you to your destination .

she smiled with tears in her eyes ,
I have no destination , she replies .
never hurt a lady , she advices .
that answer makes me surprised .

I asked , is something wrong ?
she told me her husband had left her alone .
and also taking her happiness along.
and she do not wants to live anymore.

I asked her what you will do now ?
she smiles and told me she don't know.
however I have memories my son to live ,
she left , telling how her happiness blew.

she was the daughter of eve ,
that why she was brave .

POEM 10. THE TRUTHE BEHIND MY SMILING FACE

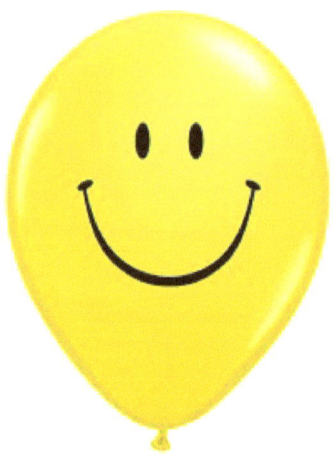

There're thousands of smiling faces,
But do you know the truth behind that,
Everyone has been tired of his fate,
Still trying hard to get over that,

When the sun rises, you can see me smiling,
But when it comes night, it's hard to stop crying,
You'll never know the truth behind my smiling face,
Just because all you can see me smiling,

Have you ever seen a fish crying?
No, you would have never seen,
Yes, she does, she shouts, when you take her out of stream,
In my case I have no stream.
Stream of happiness, not even a single drop of water.

Still trying hard to show the world,
That I am smiling, and I am not finished.
Someday I will swim in the ocean.
Ocean of the happiness, will take me in her arms.

Just because I am smiling,
Doesn't means I am happy,
It means I am strong,
Strong enough, to hide my tears.

About the Poet

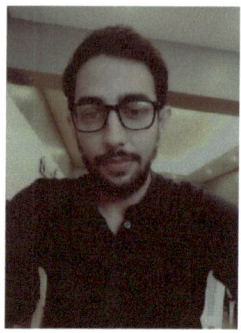

ASIM ZULFIQAR is an electronic engineer, author and a freelancer. He has been writing poem for 3 years and these are the best collection of him.

Learn more about Asim at
https://www.facebook.com/asimzulfiqar067

If you like this collection, make sure to review the book that will be appreciation for me.

www.ingramcontent.com/pod-product-compliance
Lightning Source LLC
Chambersburg PA
CBHW040351220526
45473CB00009B/2848